NATIONAL GEOGRAPHIC

Ladders

ONWARD!

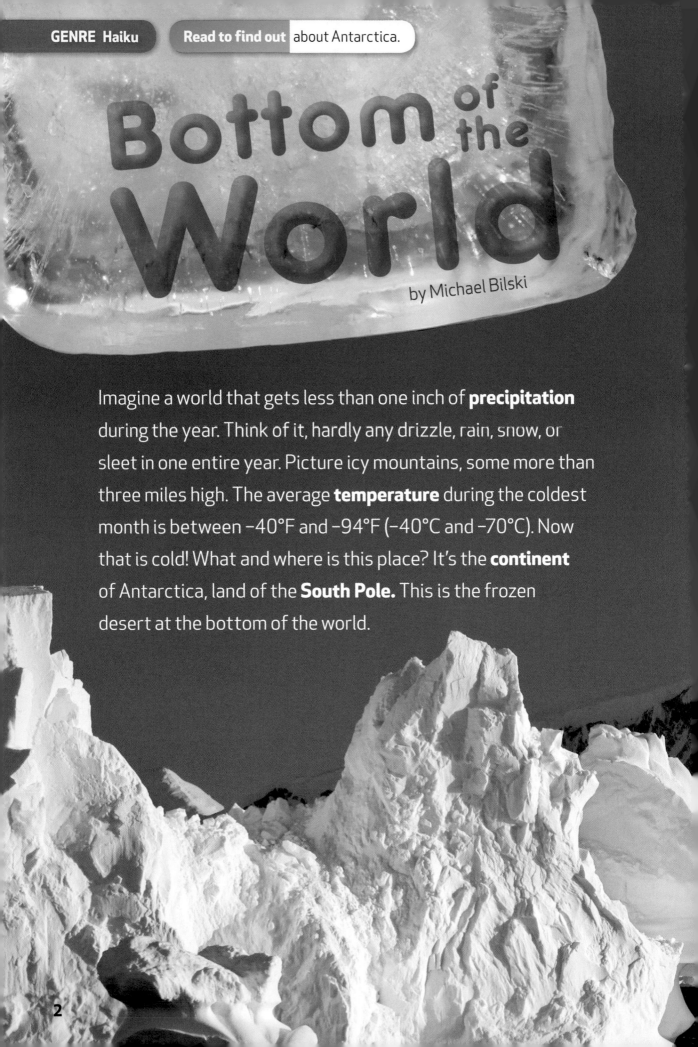

Bottom of the World

by Michael Bilski

Imagine a world that gets less than one inch of **precipitation** during the year. Think of it, hardly any drizzle, rain, snow, or sleet in one entire year. Picture icy mountains, some more than three miles high. The average **temperature** during the coldest month is between –40°F and –94°F (–40°C and –70°C). Now that is cold! What and where is this place? It's the **continent** of Antarctica, land of the **South Pole.** This is the frozen desert at the bottom of the world.

Haiku 1

Bottom of the world

Continent like no other

Stark Antarctica!

Haiku 2

World's coldest desert

Freezing in the ice and wind

Is it ever warm?

Haiku 3

Lure to explorers

Brave men who would not give up

Onward to the Pole!

Check In How would you describe Antarctica?

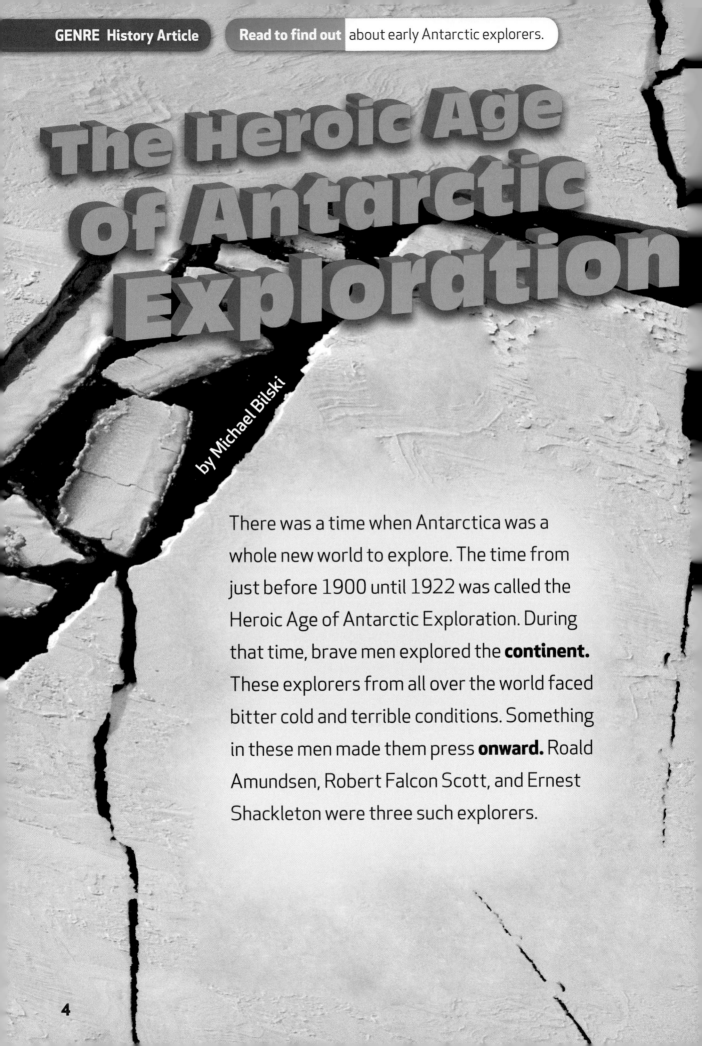

The Heroic Age of Antarctic Exploration

by Michael Bilski

There was a time when Antarctica was a whole new world to explore. The time from just before 1900 until 1922 was called the Heroic Age of Antarctic Exploration. During that time, brave men explored the **continent.** These explorers from all over the world faced bitter cold and terrible conditions. Something in these men made them press **onward.** Roald Amundsen, Robert Falcon Scott, and Ernest Shackleton were three such explorers.

Antarctic Explorers

Erich von Drygalski

German South Polar
Expedition, 1901–1903

Roald Amundsen

Norwegian Antarctic
Expedition, 1910–1912

*First to reach South Pole
(December 14, 1911)*

Adriene de Gerlache

Belgian Antarctic
Expedition, 1897–1899

William Speirs Bruce

Scottish National
Antarctic Expedition,
1902–1904

Ernest Shackleton

British Antarctic
Expedition, 1907–1909

Imperial Trans-Antarctic
Expedition, 1914–1917

Shackleton-Rowett
Expedition, 1921–1922

**Carsten
Borchgrevink**

British Antarctic
Expedition, 1898–1900

Jean-Baptiste Charcot

French Antarctic
Expedition, 1903–1905
and 1908–1910

Nobu Shirase

Japanese Antarctic
Expedition, 1910–1912

**Nils Otto
Nordenskjold**

Swedish South Polar
Expedition, 1901–1903

Robert Falcon Scott

British National Antarctic
Expedition, 1901–1904

British Antarctic
Expedition, 1910–1913

*Reached South Pole
(January 17, 1912)*

Douglas Mawson

Australasian Antarctic
Expedition, 1911–1914

5

Roald Amundsen

Roald Amundsen was born in Norway in 1872. He explored the polar Arctic region and wanted to be the first to reach the **North Pole.** In the cold north, Amundsen learned how the Inuit survived. He began to wear reindeer clothing as they did. He also learned about using sled dogs. When other explorers discovered the North Pole before Amundsen, he decided that he would be the first to reach the **South Pole.** He knew that Robert Scott had the same goal. The race was on!

Robert Falcon Scott

Robert Falcon Scott was born in England in 1868. He was barely a teen when he began his career in the navy. Scott's first **expedition** to Antarctica took place from 1901 to 1904. Scott and his team came within 400 miles of the South Pole. Scott was determined to lead the first expedition to reach the South Pole, and he returned to Antarctica in 1911. He was disappointed to learn that Amundsen had the same goal, but Scott would not give up.

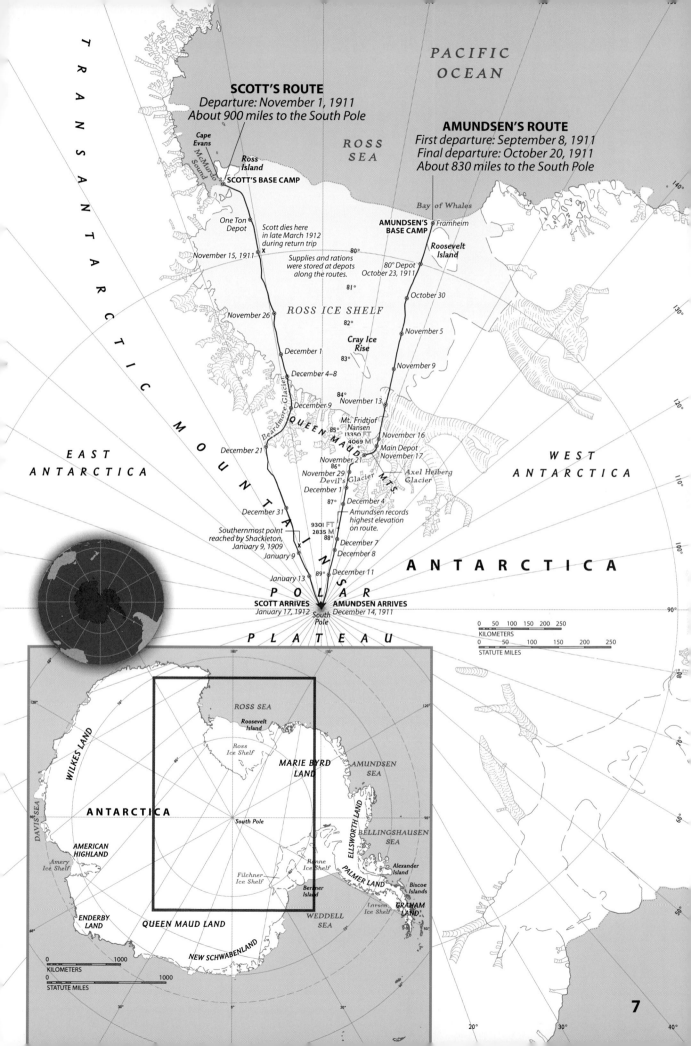

PACIFIC
OCEAN

SCOTT'S ROUTE
*Departure: November 1, 1911
About 900 miles to the South Pole*

AMUNDSEN'S ROUTE
*First departure: September 8, 1911
Final departure: October 20, 1911
About 830 miles to the South Pole*

*ROSS
SEA*

Cape
Evans

Ross
Island

SCOTT'S BASE CAMP

Bay of Whales

One Ton
Depot

Scott dies here
in late March 1912
during return trip

**AMUNDSEN'S
BASE CAMP**   *Framheim*

November 15, 1911   X

80°   *Roosevelt
Island*

*Supplies and rations
were stored at depots
along the routes.*

*80° Depot
October 23, 1911*

81°

October 30

November 26   *ROSS ICE SHELF*   *82°*

November 5

December 1   *Cray Ice
Rise*   *83°*

December 4–8   *November 9*

84°

December 9   *November 13*

*Mt. Fridtjof
Nansen
13350 FT
4069 M*   *November 16*

85°

December 21   *QUEEN MAUD*   *November 21*   *Main Depot
November 17*

86°   *Axel Heiberg
Glacier*

November 29

Devil's Glacier

December 1   *M T S.*

87°

*EAST
ANTARCTICA*

*WEST
ANTARCTICA*

December 4

*Amundsen records
highest elevation
on route.*

December 31

*9301 FT
2835 M*

*Southernmost point
reached by Shackleton,
January 9, 1909*   X   *88°*   *December 7*

December 8

January 9

89°   *December 11*

January 13

A N T A R C T I C A

P O L A R

SCOTT ARRIVES   **AMUNDSEN ARRIVES**
January 17, 1912   *December 14, 1911*
*South
Pole*

P L A T E A U

0 50 100 150 200 250
KILOMETERS
0   50   100   150   200   250
STATUTE MILES

T R A N S A N T A R C T I C   M O U N T A I N S

180°

ROSS SEA

Roosevelt
Island

Ross
Ice Shelf

MARIE BYRD
LAND

AMUNDSEN
SEA

WILKES LAND

DAVIS
SEA

ANTARCTICA

South Pole

90°

BELLINGSHAUSEN
SEA

AMERICAN
HIGHLAND

ELLSWORTH LAND

Alexander
Island

Amery
Ice Shelf

Ronne
Ice Shelf

PALMER LAND

Biscoe
Islands

ENDERBY
LAND

Filchner
Ice Shelf

Berkner
Island

WEDDELL
SEA

Larsen
Ice Shelf

GRAHAM
LAND

QUEEN MAUD LAND

NEW SCHWABENLAND

0   1000
KILOMETERS
0   1000
STATUTE MILES

Fram

Amundsen

Amundsen

The Pole Is the Goal

Amundsen and Scott shared a goal. Each wanted to be the first explorer to reach the South Pole. Planning and luck would both play a role in deciding the winner of this race.

On January 3, 1911, Scott and his **crew** arrived in Antarctica on their ship, *Terra Nova*. Although they lost some cargo during a storm at sea, Scott's team came supplied with dogs, ponies, and gasoline-powered sleds. Before setting off for the South Pole, Scott and his men set up **depots** to store food and supplies along the route to the Pole. However, one of the gasoline-powered sleds broke down, and the ponies struggled in the bitter cold. The team could not set up their main depot as far south as they had hoped.

Terra Nova

Scott

Scott

Sled at a supply depot

On January 14, 1911, Amundsen and his crew arrived in Antarctica on their ship, *Fram*. They set up base camp on the Ross Ice Shelf. They would stay there for nine months, preparing for the trek to the South Pole.

Amundsen was prepared with supplies and fresh water. He remembered what he had learned from the Inuit. He knew skis and dogs would help him in his quest. He brought almost 100 sled dogs to Antarctica. Amundsen and his crew spent weeks moving supplies and food from *Fram* to the camp. They set up depots with food along the trail to the Pole. As the men waited for the weather to improve in spring, they practiced and prepared. They trained the dogs. They practiced skiing. The men used the trained dogs and sleds to get their supply depots closer to the Pole than Scott could. Amundsen also made sure his men and dogs were well-fed and rested for the trip ahead.

Dog team

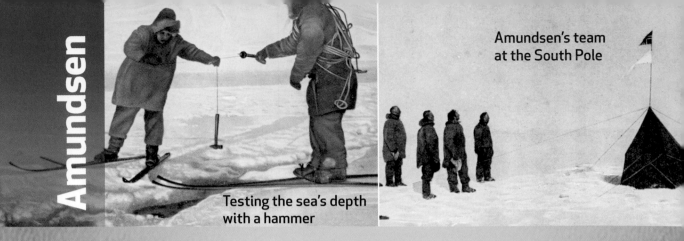

Testing the sea's depth
with a hammer

Amundsen's team
at the South Pole

Victory and Defeat

On October 20, 1911, Amundsen set off for the South Pole.
His crew included a champion skier and two expert dog
drivers. They took four sleds and more than 50 dogs. The
food depots did the trick. The men skied and the dogs pulled
the sleds. The team used stones to mark the trail. Climbing
mountains and battling blizzards, the frostbitten men and
dogs pressed onward. Finally, on December 14, 1911, they
reached the Pole! There was no sign of Scott. The race was
won. Amundsen and his men celebrated their victory. They
planted a flag and set up a tent. Inside the tent, Amundsen
left a note for Scott.

Scott left base camp on November 1, 1911. With him and
his crew were 10 ponies, sleds, and more than 20 dogs. The
gasoline-powered sleds failed. The ponies struggled in the
ice and snow. The team faced bitter cold and endless snow.
A blizzard held them up for four days. Scott's team had to

Both explorers chose their teams and equipment differently.

AMUNDSEN'S TEAM   ■ Survived trip   □ Did not survive

SCOTT'S TEAM

As planned, these men turned back
before reaching the South Pole.

The total number of sleds is uncertain. Two
were brought back by returning men.

Crossing a glacier on foot

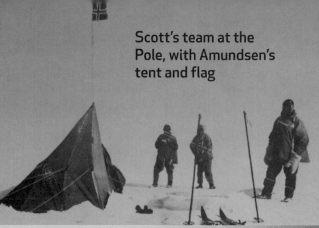
Scott's team at the Pole, with Amundsen's tent and flag

march on foot. They were not capable skiers, and they had to pull their own sleds. As they traveled toward the South Pole, Scott sent the dogs and most of the men back to base camp. He decided to take four men the rest of the way. On January 16, 1912, they saw something that made their hearts sink. In the distance, Amundsen's tent and flag came into view. They knew they had lost the race. When they reached the South Pole on January 17, they found what Amundsen had left for them, including some much-needed supplies.

Amundsen and his team had made it back safely, but Scott's team was less fortunate. They were starving, ill, and exhausted. The remaining men were trapped by a blizzard, 11 miles from their largest depot. They never made it there. Scott's final diary entry finished the sad story.

"We shall stick it out to the end, but we are getting weaker, of course, and the end cannot be far. It seems a pity, but I do not think I can write more."

All surviving dogs were brought back by returning team members.

Shackleton's Endurance

Ernest Henry Shackleton

Ernest Henry Shackleton was born in 1874 in Ireland. He was a member of Scott's crew during Scott's first attempt to reach the South Pole in 1901. In 1908, Shackleton led his own expedition and set a record by getting closer to the South Pole than anyone had before that time.

After Amundsen won the race to the South Pole, Shackleton decided to try something new. He would cross Antarctica on foot. The plan was to start from the Weddell Sea

Sled dogs watch *Endurance* sink.

This map traces their route.

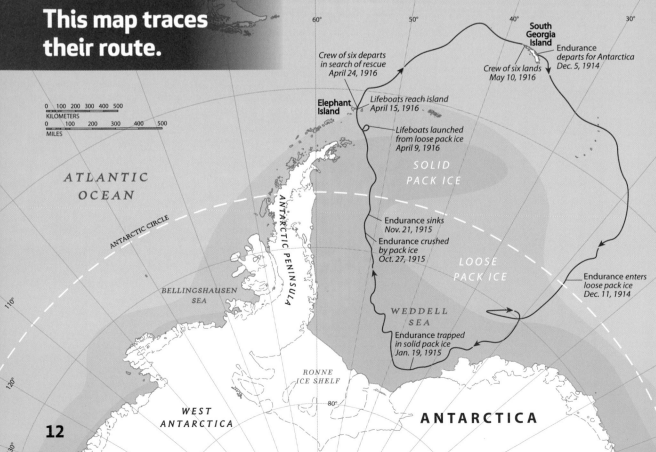

Crew of six departs in search of rescue
April 24, 1916

South Georgia Island

Endurance departs for Antarctica
Dec. 5, 1914

Crew of six lands
May 10, 1916

Elephant Island

Lifeboats reach island
April 15, 1916

Lifeboats launched from loose pack ice
April 9, 1916

SOLID PACK ICE

0 100 200 300 400 500
KILOMETERS
0 100 200 300 400 500
MILES

ATLANTIC OCEAN

ANTARCTIC CIRCLE

ANTARCTIC PENINSULA

BELLINGSHAUSEN SEA

Endurance *sinks*
Nov. 21, 1915

Endurance *crushed*
by pack ice
Oct. 27, 1915

LOOSE PACK ICE

Endurance *enters*
loose pack ice
Dec. 11, 1914

WEDDELL SEA

Endurance *trapped*
in solid pack ice
Jan. 19, 1915

RONNE ICE SHELF

WEST ANTARCTICA

ANTARCTICA

and cross a completely unexplored region of Antarctica. The expedition would head to the Pole and then to the Ross Sea.

Shackleton and his men spotted Antarctica. Before Shackleton reached Antarctica, his ship, *Endurance*, became trapped in a drifting pack ice. It was a fatal blow to the expedition. For ten long months, the pack ice held the ship in its powerful clutches. Meanwhile Shackleton and his men used *Endurance* as their base and storage facility. But the ice was slowly crushing the doomed ship, and supplies and lifeboats eventually had to be removed. On November 21, 1915, *Endurance* was crushed and later sank.

Still trapped on the dangerous pack ice, Shackleton and his crew drifted for another five months. The men and dogs endured bitter cold. They survived partly on whale and seal meat. Finally, in their small lifeboats, Shackleton's men were able to escape the ice and get safely to Elephant Island.

Shackleton and his men were trapped on the ice. They didn't set foot on land for more than a year.

Shackleton decided the only hope for rescue was to get one of the lifeboats to the open sea and sail to the nearest inhabited island. It was a dangerous mission. With a crew of five men, Shackleton sailed 800 miles to South Georgia Island. There, they found a ship that could bring them back to rescue the remaining crew. After several unsuccessful attempts, every member of Shackleton's expedition was finally rescued on August 30, 1916. The men had been away from home for more than two years.

The expedition was a failure, but the story of *Endurance* had a heroic end. True to the name of their ship, Shackleton and his fellow explorers had endured.

In 1921 Shackleton reunited with some members of the *Endurance* crew. The plan was to sail a new ship, *Quest*, all the way around Antarctica. Shackleton suffered a heart attack while on board *Quest*. He was buried on South Georgia Island.

Shackleton's crew on board *Quest*

End of the Heroic Age

Shackleton's death marked the end of this heroic age. The final continent had been explored, and both Amundsen and Scott had reached the South Pole. Exploration of a different kind continues to this day. Scientists from all over the world have set up research stations to study this frozen land.

Endurance

Check In   What did Scott, Amundsen, and Shackleton have in common? How were they different?

Andrew
Evans

Meet Andrew Evans, National Geographic's "Digital Nomad." A nomad is a traveler, which is what Andrew is. He's a digital nomad because he uses technology to communicate about his travels.

Andrew wanted to explore **Antarctica**, much like the explorers of the Heroic Age of Antarctic Exploration. Instead of sailing to Antarctica, Andrew traveled most of the way by bus. People followed Andrew's journey on his **blog**. He kept busy posting news for them every day.

Andrew's
Antarctic Adventure

by Michael Bilski

In the first decades of the 20th century, the explorers Amundsen, Scott, and Shackleton used navigation instruments, such as a compass and sextant, to find their way toward the **South Pole**. They recorded their journeys using large box cameras.

Andrew and other explorers today have tools that use GPS, which stands for "Global Positioning System." GPS receivers, digital cameras, and the Internet help explorers find their way and keep a record of their journey. Andrew travels light, but he always takes several small cameras with him, including a favorite waterproof one.

Tools

Present	Past

Cell-phone compass	*Compass*

GPS receiver	*Sextant*

Waterproof camera	*Box camera*

Heading South

On January 1, 2010, Andrew got on the bus outside the National Geographic offices in Washington, D.C. Before beginning his long journey, Andrew had asked blog readers to help him pick songs for the ultimate playlist. The songs helped pass the time on the long ride.

ATLANTIC OCEAN

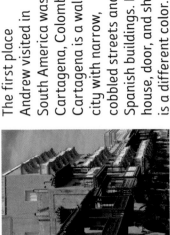

The first place Andrew visited in South America was Cartagena, Colombia. Cartagena is a walled city with narrow, cobbled streets and old Spanish buildings. Every house, door, and shutter is a different color.

VENEZUELA

COLOMBIA

ECUADOR

UNITED STATES

MEXICO

BELIZE

GUATEMALA

HONDURAS

EL SALVADOR

NICARAGUA

COSTA RICA

PANAMA

In Costa Rica, Andrew saw mountain streams, macaws, toucans, and crocodiles, all from his

The sunny beaches Andrew hoped to see along the Mexican coastline were gray and colorless because of rain. But he did see white egrets and purple-black grackles.

The road in and out of La Paz, Bolivia, was over 13,500 feet in elevation. That's more than two miles high! In Southern Bolivia, Andrew saw the spectacular Uyuni salt flats. These flats make up the world's largest salt desert.

PARAG

URUGUAY

BOLIVIA

ARGENTINA

CHILE

PACIFIC
OCEAN

Ecuador is where Andrew crossed the **Equator**. He walked along the line between North and South, with one foot in each hemisphere.

When Andrew crossed the border from Ecuador to Peru, the land changed from a tropical jungle to a desert. Here the Sechura Desert meets the Pacific Ocean to the west and the Andes Mountains to the east.

The final bus ride through Argentina was more than 3100 miles. Andrew traveled through Cordoba, then **onward** to Ushuaia in Tierra del Fuego. Rough seas in the Strait of Magellan made the short ferry ride pretty scary.

Antarctica at Last

No more buses! Andrew boarded the MV National Geographic Explorer to sail to Antarctica. An afternoon highlight was seeing a pod of fin whales in front of the ship. Andrew saw his first iceberg, too. A good start to Antarctica!

ATLANTIC OCEAN

ANTARCTICA

ARGENTINA

CHILE

Andrew set foot on Antarctica. Its stark beauty touched him. He felt happy that he was able to leave his boot prints on the soil of the seventh **continent.**

Andrew visited Deception Island, a volcanic crown hollowed out from the inside. The whole island is the mouth of a volcano. On the beach at Deception Island, Andrew did something unusual. He went for a swim. Since the water was 36°F (2°C), he didn't stay in long.

On the island of South Georgia, Andrew snapped this picture of a very rare all-black penguin. Its rare coloring is called melanism. Melanism happens when increased melanin in the body causes dark pigmentation on the skin, fur, or feathers.

The rules for visitors to Antarctica say that you cannot touch any wildlife. You need to stay 15 feet away from the animals at all times. On a visit to the Gentoo penguin colony at Port Lockroy, a baby penguin jumped into Andrew's lap. Then another one came. It was all he could do to obey the rules and not cuddle the penguins.

Andrew traveled through 14 countries and covered 10,000 miles in 10 weeks! His trip began on a bus in Washington, D.C. It ended on the continent of Antarctica.

Andrew, like the explorers of the Heroic Age of Antarctic Exploration, set his sights on a destination. He dealt with bumps along the way, but he always managed to press onward. It's what explorers do.

Check In What did you find most interesting about Andrew's trip?

Discuss Compare and Contrast

1. What do you think connects the three pieces that you read in this book? What makes you think that?

2. Compare and contrast the reasons why Amundsen, Scott, Shackleton, and Evans went to Antarctica. How were their reasons alike and different?

3. Andrew Evans uses modern tools, such as a GPS device and a cell phone. How might modern tools have changed the other explorers' expeditions?

4. Choose a haiku. Then find a passage or a photo in another piece that explains or shows what the haiku is describing. Tell how they are connected.

5. What questions do you still wonder about Antarctica or its explorers?